ANNETTE HAYN
CHAMBER MUSIC

NEW & SELECTED POEMS

THE POET'S PRESS
Pittsburgh, PA

Copyright © 2001, 2009 by The Poet's Press
All Rights Reserved
Second Edition, Expanded

Some of the poems in this book have appeared in
Extensions, Glassworks, The Painted Bride,
Antenna, Telephone,
Poets Fortnightly, Caprice and *The Villanelle*

Book design by Brett Rutherford

This is the 179th publication of
THE POET'S PRESS
2209 Murray Avenue #3
Pittsburgh, PA 15217
www.poetspress.org
Paperback: ISBN 0-922558-37-X

This book is also available
in Adobe Acrobat format.

TABLE OF CONTENTS

Annette Hayn: A Memoir, by Mary Ferrari   xi

CHAMBER MUSIC
Exits   17
Chamber Music   18
Ghost Ship   19
The Rehearsal   20
Famous Poets   21
Mortality   22
Abstract Art   23
An Evening of Disguises   25
The Players   27
Standstill   28
An Evening Song   29
House Hunting   31
Birthday Night   33
Tides   34
The Twelve Birds   35

RUMORS ABOUT HEAVEN
Noah's Wife   39
Of Accidents and Forests   41
On Holidays I Don't Observe   42
The Decision   43
The Blessing of the Animals   44
The Girl Who Hid from Death   45
A Place of Rituals   46
Variations on Los Angeles   47
The Rescued   48
Before the Rain   49
Afraid of Standing Still   50
Eve   52
In Transit   53
The Door   55
Rumors About Heaven   56

FAIRY TALE UPDATE
    The Birthday Book 59
    A Paved Forest 60
    Mary's House 62
    Dry Spell 63
    Ice Trees 64
    Cradle Song 65
    Threatened by Toys 66
    Constant Danger 68
    Catherine's Forest 69
    Tower Door 70
    The Window Washer 72
    A Private Plane 73
    Winter Interval 74
    Scenes from a Wedding 75
    Witches Passing By 78

SELECTED POEMS
    From *Rapunzel (1971)*
        Frances 81
        The Woods 82
        The Tower 82
        Rapunzel 83
        As Well As Nights 83
        The Weekend 84
    From *One-Armed Flyer (1976)*
        December Street Scene 85
        Unlikely Marriage 86
        The Way You Are 87
        Lullaby 98
    From *Journeys Around One Point (1980)*
        Young Girl Sleeping Late 89
        Sailboat 90
    From *The Crossing (1984)*
        Pack of Dogs 94
        Imagined Rain 95
        Colonial Doll House 96
        Doll Houses 97
    From *Calendar House (1990)*
        Painted Windows 99
        Calendar House 100

The Semi-Conscious Bride   102
From *Enemy on the Way to School (1994)*
  The Island   104
  High Holy Day   105
  Where Dragons Sang   106
  Marianne   108

MEMORIAL TO THE MOON
  Third Act   111
  Phyllis's Funeral   112
  Chemo Marathon   113
  Prelude to a Beheading   114
  Sonata   115
  Absence 2   116
  Assistant Gods   117
  The Album   118
  Memorial to the Moon   119
  Watercolors   120
  Outlines   120
  Family Tree   121
  Ceremonies in White   122
  To a Teenager   124
  Drought   125
  Visit   126
  Revolving Door   127
  Inside-Out   128
  Notes on Growing Up   129
  Tree Shadows   131
  Basement Mirror   132
  The Lamp Breaks   132
  A Shelter Story   133
  Reclassified   134
  Interlude   135
  Indoor Duet   136
  The Curtain   137
  Call Waiting   138
  The New Millennium   139
  Fall 2001   140
  Storyteller   141
  Bluebird Flowers   142
  For Kathie   143

Wilderness   144
Password   145
Heaven   146
Gabriela   147
Rendezvous   148
Gerry Waiting   149

About the Author   150
About This Book   151

CHAMBER
MUSIC

For Anna

ANNETTE HAYN: A MEMOIR

Annette Hayn and I met in late September of 1964, almost exactly forty years before the day she died, September 30, 2004. As a suburban wife and mother, I felt intimidated when I walked into the classroom at the New School where Kenneth Koch's poetry workshop would soon begin. A woman with a friendly smile was sitting in the back row, so I sat down next to her. I looked around the room and decided that the rest of the students were probably Greenwich Village swingers.

For Annette and me, Kenneth Koch's workshop proved to be the beginning of our lives as poets and the start of a friendship that lasted until her death.

Kenneth Koch was a charismatic teacher and an innovative poet who proved to be an inspiring influence on us and on many others. We made other important friends in his workshop as well, Catherine Murray and Frances Waldman among them. Over the years we frequently quoted Kenneth Koch's teachings and referred often in conversations to other poets, especially but not only the leaders of the New York avant garde of the 20th century: Frank O'Hara, John Ashbery, James Schuyler, and of course the great poets: Whitman, Dickinson, Lorca, Stephens among them.

Annette and I read each other's poems, offering detailed criticism, the same kind of line-by-line criticism that Kenneth Koch had given us. A phone would ring. Annette would say, "Do you have a minute? I'm working on a new poem and it's driving me crazy." For her part, Annette's editorial skills enhanced many of my poems, although she was too modest to make such a claim. We talked about our lives and families. Annette found a way to attend my son John and Jodie's wedding in Poughkeepsie, and Frank and I went to Debbie and Phil's wonderful wedding in Amagansett.

To Annette, references to Catholicism in my poems was not off-putting but intriguing. I was impressed by poems about her childhood as a Jewish girl in Nazi Germany and thought those poems were among her best. They were written without melodrama, as just one part of her life. I consider her collection, *Enemy on the Way to School*, as her most powerful book.

Two weeks before she died of cancer, Annette called me and said, "Mary, get to work on your next book! I'd love to help you with it!" Despite the extremity of her illness, her enthusiasm for this project was amazing.

Memorial to the Moon, the last section of this new expanded edition of Annette's *Chamber Music,* is a wonderful posthumous collection of Annette's work. The title-poem exemplifies the theme of mutability at odds with the fast-paced images in a lyrical game of hide-and-seek at the beginning:

>The moon goes underground.
>Veiled flowers run and hide.
>The stars wear masks.
>The mountains are disguised.

"Memorial to the Moon," like many of the poems in this collection, becomes poignant at the end: "The candles flicker for miles/ For all things I can't find."

"For Kathie," Annette's most delightful poem, begins meditatively:

>Some old people seek the sun
>As if it won't recur,
>Not in their lifetimes,
>But I stay home
>And rediscover Kathie.

The third stanza has immediacy: "But open the door, and there/ She is, carrying bags/ of groceries for me." This poem also concludes wistfully: "The minutes run away/ And I chase after them./ Let me keep this one/ Just a little longer." I admire the way she combines meditation, joy, and the urgency of time so convincingly in one short poem. Each stanza has a radically different tone, without losing a developing sense of the whole experience.

"Ceremonies in White" is a complex poem notable for its smooth intermingling of themes and images, a joyous wedding and the devastation of war, reminiscent of W.H. Auden's "Musée des Beaux Arts." The end of the poem expresses the paradox of life:

Cameras catch everyone,
Wedding guests arriving,
Soldiers recovering,
The couple lifted high,
So temporary, so promising —

Six bridesmaids wearing black,
One spring night dressed in snow.

In the last five months of Annette's life our frequent communications were by phone. Her voice and her poems continued to be vibrant. In "Gerry Waiting" she imagines her late husband greeting her in the afterlife. She writes, "will he show me around?" Due to her matter-of-fact tone, I didn't understand that her death was imminent. A unique poem, "Chemo-Marathon," written several years before she died, is a surreal treatment of her experience with chemotherapy. It begins "Good knights and bad knights battle in my veins." Toward the end, she writes: "Death and hope walk through the/ forest, making bets. The tycoon/ is never happy. The raccoon/ still wears white socks." The tycoon and the raccoon symbolize death and hope. Most post-modern poets that I've read write realistic poems about experiences with disease, whereas Annette's poem has a playful tone.

She learned from Kenneth Koch to avoid self-pity and sentimentality. And she remained herself: inventive, witty, and true to her own unique history and visionary mode.

— *Mary Ferrari*
February 2009

CHAMBER MUSIC

Exits

After sharing the bathtub
with drowning ants
I attempt a graceful exit.

Can each life revise the universe
the way future rovers
may revise Mars?

I marvel at the cleverness
of Jeopardy contestants.
But what about unfathomable

questions, the saints who
disappear under the earth,
their non-return?

I've missed my exit, so
I'm growing old. In windless seas
the sailboats are asleep.

A group of children passes me
on their way to a restaurant
in the next century.

Lightning disrupts a field of fireflies.
Each of their moments is eternity,
their wedding on a borrowed planet.

Chamber Music

Through the new window
a parade of light bulbs strips the trees.
I see the musicians coming

"You're always in a bad mood
when the musicians come,"
Gerry used to say.

Music stands define the inner circle.
No one may speak or fall asleep.
Violins disrupt my privacy.
A viola transcends the family.

I'm jealous of musicians
who steal my scene and play forever.
The musicians are coming

This morning darkness but
no rain. I hear Gerry whistle
(the family whistle)
watch him approach under an umbrella —

When the umbrella closes
he's someone else.

Beyond the new window
he sleeps through my story.
The truth outlasts the hero.
Musician, stop ignoring me!

No one may break the spell or die.
The musicians are coming.

Ghost Ship

1
By now a lake has formed
around the linden tree
on the front lawn.
Surrounded by white walls
I feel the passion
of the rain that I'm not in.

2
We're always in two places:
the bed and the dream,
this moment and far away,
this room and another year.

3
On the balcony of an opera house
we used to feel so safe
in other people's lives.

Having just met we knew we were
in love, but then a vengeful clown
removed my veil. You turned into
the Flying Dutchman, departed
on a ghost ship —

I can no longer find you when
the lights go on.

The Rehearsal

The rehearsal was not satisfactory
The characters said the right words
But under the influence of thunder
They couldn't manage the silences

The characters said the right words
But they forgot to listen
They couldn't manage the silences
"Show more anger   Throw her to the ground"

But they forgot to listen
To undercurrents of the past
"Show more anger   Throw her to the ground
Give her a reason to react"

The undercurrents of the past
The play I wasn't allowed to see
Give her a reason to react
I envied members of the cast

The play I wasn't allowed to see
(I can't forget the imagined scenery)
I envied members of the cast
Who stepped on each other's lines

I can't forget the imagined scenery
But raindrops kept intruding
Stepped on each other's lines
On a return trip to the river

Raindrops kept intruding
Under the influence of thunder
On a return trip to the river —
The rehearsal was not satisfactory

Famous Poets

A famous poet has agreed
to listen to our poetry reading.
Kenneth Koch says, "You're very lucky."
Is he the famous poet?
We decide to read one poem each.
Famous poets don't stick around for long.

I want Mary to make the introductions
but let her decline for someone better known.
In the mirror I don't like myself
so I put on a lot of lipstick.

The room is crowded, not with people
but equipment. I am allowed
to ride in a car that sometimes
leaves the road to fly above the traffic.
But I have to sit in the back with a dog.
Only famous poets sit in front.

Mortality

Waiting for my ride
I saw a giant bird
like a king

about to be dethroned
high in the storm
got dizzy watching it

so I fell down the steps
of the medical building —
That bird stood on a branch

in its own blackness
swinging back and forth
There were no leaves

to mask its disappearance —
The drops of blood astonished me
The taxi wouldn't wait

Abstract Art

When the bedroom ceiling looks
like abstract art
and plaster falls into
your sleep

paint your house into a palace.
(Dilute the green)
Place the palace in a forest.
(No one will cut those trees.)

Paint the faces of the old
young again. Paint the
devil disoriented,
the fugitive disguised.

If you are afraid of falling
paint the fall. If you can't walk
paint yourself walking.
Paint the room you were evicted from.

A popular portrait painter
adds missing hair, adoring dogs,
anything to help his subjects
like themselves.

Be selective about topics.
Paint the man you married
but not his death.
Paint him sightseeing at every stop

then running for the train
that you are in
each time almost missing it
and you without a passport.

Paint a storm, how it dissolves
the lawn. Watch out! under your feet!
Don't trip over the lizard's tail.
Paint it.

If the day has been imperfect
(A computer mixed the colors)
you'll get to like it
when it dries.

An Evening of Disguises

1
The moon got tired
of her monthly routine
yellow and pale
through centuries of lovers —
She never played the lead
so she decided to
transform herself   to become
gaudy and irregular
in iridescent colors —
People who saw her
were surprised

2
"Look at that moon!" on the way home
from Christmas dinner.
"What moon? — You mean
this huge, lopsided egg?"

The moon looks too unreal
to be believed onstage
The characters we play
grow old then young

3
Christmas is one tradition
I wish I were entitled to —
unexpected angels
from a foreign realm

(When Gerry brought home
our first Christmas tree
our small daughter cried so hard
he had to take it back)

hidden inside a riddle
behind a chair
or fastened to the skyline
like that moon

The Players

Nobody likes Lisa.
She is cast as
the fat girl in the play
about a troubled family.

The father yells. Lisa looks
for food. He beats the son
throws down his wife
while Lisa snacks.

She acts aggressively
in every scene.
We complain —
feel sad when she is fired.

Now I play the fat girl.
The director asks, "Are you
comfortable in the part?"
I keep on eating.

Father says, "You'll never pass
for fat." Brother says, "Instead
of *Fatso* I'll call you *Ugly*."
Mother says, "You have a lovely face."

STANDSTILL

In this garden without trees
words lose their wings.
Nothing can be resolved,
not the anger, not the flower.

In this garden without trees
the mother does not know
she's ill, nor can
the father find his way.

In this garden without trees
the child is disguised
as a moody moon, visible
but out of reach.

An Evening Song

Restore the German snow,
Retrace the teachers' footsteps
To where a student was excluded
From the singing,
Isolated on the lower branches,
Forced to recite what no one understood.

It's important to understand
How minute snowflakes
Have the power to wound branches,
How they affect the footsteps
Of an opera singer
Leaving her voiceless and excluded.

Some of the excluded
Are hard to understand.
With no audience they keep on singing.
The lark won't let the moods of snow
Destroy its footsteps
On Shakespearean branches.

Underneath fast burning branches
(Some trees have been excluded)
Look for the soldiers' footsteps,
Their cause misunderstood.
In the forgiving snow
They destroy and they sing.

All day the lark keeps singing
Despite the ruined branches,
The bloodstained snow.
But the wolf has been excluded.
Can you understand
The sadness of losing one's footsteps?

A spurned Ophelia steps
Into madness for her final song.
Her dark fate helps us understand
River images branching
From realms of exclusion,
Floating flowers untouched by snow.

Snowy footsteps are excluded
From the singing in the branches,
Their destination not understood.

House Hunting

1
They are selecting scenery
for a play that's not yet written.
Will there be flowers for the deer to eat?
Is the den too dark for a wake up scene?
Where will the woods reside?

Can they find extras in a nearby street,
a despondent daisy or abandoned cat?
Some scenes may need more characters,
but it's not easy to get pregnant
in this whirlwind of decisions.

How far do clouds commute
to a farmhouse in the 18th century,
a stone cottage with restricted light?
Will they repaint the moody sky, can they
afford it, the influence of rivers,
their words and eyes?

2
Last night I returned to the house
I lived in years ago
(I still have the key)
in order to complete a poem.

Every weekend the children
search for the perfect house.
Promising ones are in drab towns
far from the river.

Looking for the perfect poem
I keep returning to the wrong house,
no longer sure where I live.
I hear footsteps of the present.

Turn off the light! ... Hide!

3
They buy a former icehouse
bridging two centuries
next to a pond.
A newly arrived moon
swims towards them.
This story has a waterfall
of walls and trees,
fish naming scenes
and owners become slaves.
What if house dreams
of mowing moonlit slopes,
what if they tire
and give way to doubt,
what if exhilaration —

Birthday Night

Held hostage on
a remote third floor
I try to fall asleep
It starts to snow

Feeling elated
excluded and afraid
I can't unlock
the window to this snow

Lined up below
the stairs turn into years
new sleeping families
new snow-swept trees

If I could manage
to climb down
three doors would open —
Everyone's awake

Once outside
they switch identities
the captured garden
war horses of snow

Tides

1
An ancestor in a painting leaves
for a museum in New York.
He scrutinizes visitors,
then at night when no one's looking
returns to his own century.

2
Vacation time, a time to leave.
Departing swans glazed with new rain
in Africa, Thailand and Spain,
reluctant to return.

3
Sleep long, return to normal.
Pay a return visit to the doctor. Leave
with a new disease. Return to
the mirror but only in the dark.
Return to dark birds like drops of rain.

4
Return to the beginning,
you playing in the orchestra,
I in the front row listening.
A girl on stage gets stabbed. Don't leave
me in the middle of the aria.

5
With everyone on a journey
it's time to leave in your own sailboat.
Look in on a honeymoon in Thailand.
Stay overnight in a bright memory.
Return to preparations for the wedding.

The Twelve Birds

1
I wanted to stay forever
in the moment of the birth.
The clock ticked unobtrusively.
Every hour it played the song
of the twelve birds.

2
In a ski hut with my mother
anticipating the descent.
I realized I was I in the
moment of the unnamed debt.
We skied past locked lakes, unlisted
winds. The moon rolled downhill
blocking our path. A butterfly
devoured her and white birds crashed.

3
Where do you live this moment?
I live in a compartment on a train
to Canada on our honeymoon.
1 didn't like my wedding dress,
am looking for a coat for my new husband.
Why did you sneeze during the ceremony?
The men's department is uncharted territory.
Do you promise to love music now and forever?

RUMORS
ABOUT
HEAVEN

NOAH'S WIFE

1
I didn't think it was a good
idea to build an ark.
Noah would not explain.
He followed orders, expected
me to do the same.

He heard the voice of God
I only heard the wind.
He saw celestial visions
I saw nothing but fog.
He held God's trust
I needed to be held.

Imagine the commotion
in the meadow,
the stacks of wood
disturbing our view.
Neighbors jeered
and sheep were running wild.

Were the voices Noah heard
only in his head?

2
Time for the animals
to come aboard.
I liked the way
they walked in
two by two
trusting each other
and their fate
as if they heard
the voices Noah heard.

Two deer arrived.
Two butterflies flew in.
Elephants came
and took up too much room.
A lion growled at me.

When rats ran in
then crocodiles
and snakes
I was convinced
they would devour us.

3
Suddenly we were afloat, battered
by waterfalls. Two friends
passed by, disappeared.
The moon went into hiding.
Houses flew by, dispossessed
roofs, unfinished sentences.
Whole kingdoms sank.

Why was I spared? I asked too
many questions, doubted God.
Since no one knew where we were going
there was no need to steer.
Persistent lullabies of rain
kept us dazed throughout the storm.
I did not want the ark to land.

Of Accidents and Forests

A beautiful opossum
about to be run over
stands still.

The forest floor keeps shifting.
Some orphans are adopted
others swept away
haphazardly.

Future babies circle the house.
Buried relatives
call on the phone.
A great-great-grandfather
climbs out of a painting.

My dead friend Catherine
appears in the dream
in which I have to take a test
on the part Chemistry plays
in Shakespeare's tragedies.

My husband had
a ticket for *Othello*
but he got ill and died
and couldn't use it.
It is the story

of accidents and forests.
God does his gardening
haphazardly.

On Holidays I Don't Observe

In order to placate
an ever growing population
God had to allocate
some of his tasks to angels:

dark silhouettes in a white sky,
the dead who never truly died,
someone next door unrecognized,
the rescuers and referees.

On holidays I don't observe
I tell myself their stories,
ignoring gurus, rabbis, priests,
the rigid and exclusive.

Each ritual is the only
true one. Each crowded wind,
in one prescribed direction,
shouts its demanding song.

And God, besieged,
with a celestial headache —
What will become of Him?

The Decision

When the moon lay bleeding
at the bottom of a lake
and still another species
became extinct
God decided to erase the world

He should have done it sooner —
When Adam and Eve became greedy
when Samson tied the foxes
tail to tail
when birds were made of steel

Whenever God looked at the world
he couldn't bear to let it go —
He liked the varied species
planting each other
sharing their views

the forest monkeys calling out
"How light green it is
how promising —
but if you don't remember me
it never happened"

God has admired the earth
the way the woman
admires the embroidered tablecloth
with frayed forget-me-nots —
"Have you slept long enough

among the mirrors of the kingdom?"
Perhaps he'll try again.

The Blessing of the Animals

Inside the sanctuary
a woman keeps untangling
the snake around her neck

If they were surrounded
by a sudden forest
if the lurking candles
turned into jungle eyes
would the snake remember

It isn't easy being born
a snake with a history
of having tempted Eve —
This one was brought to church
to be blessed

It has a pointy vulnerable
face — The woman has no
memorable features

The Girl Who Hid from Death

All her life she has avoided
the dying and the dead.
When asked to funerals she found
excuses in the morning air,

let herself be led away
from her own dying mother
to hide among the landmarks
of her house.

While working as a nurse
whenever Death came near
she found something to do
at the other end of the ward.

What a macabre game
of hide and seek. —
When Death confronted her at last
she found she liked him,

his eyes transparent, calm
his voice a chanting stream,
the kind she used to wade in
as a child.

She touched his cloak of rain,
his hand of night,
and said, "Take me away." —
"Since you have spurned me,"

answered Death, "and hidden from me,
I will hide from you."
And he condemned her to
an endless life.

A Place of Rituals

for Gerry

You have a way
of popping out of dreams
to take over

The cemetery you are in
has its own religion
Does it still matter

the underground intrigues
the people dressed as skeletons
even after Halloween

This place of rituals is hard
to find — I have
a reservation next to yours

a reunion held at bay —
The importance of roots
to go on with their lives

Do you have travel plans
Are you still going places
without moving your feet

Variations on Los Angeles

The rioters are coming
down the avenue —
Moonlight
An ever changing view
Filtering it
is up to you

Enlarge the violet
Reduce the wound
Erase the garbage
Magnify the stars
Add would-be mountains
and a touch of snow

The graffiti
depict a polluted heaven
and its inhabitants
a burning store
in the middle
of the old testament

The snake is not to blame
for tempting Eve —
Snowmen in the path of fire
each juror brings
forbidden fruit and prayer
his version of the truth

The Rescued

A new-born boy named Moses
pulled out of the river,
a baby crow named Homer
picked up from the grass.

"The world has enough people,
enough crows."

Needy and determined
— Moses in a palace
Homer in a box —
they play hide and seek
among the columns and the thorns.

Not yet certain of his mission
not yet able to use wings
Moses follows God into the desert
Homer tags behind a woman
stands on her foot.

Before the Rain

A reckless sky
a hopeful lawn
branches impatient in the wings

In Rilke's story
the children lose a thimble
which they believe is God

With all my images
turning a wilted brown
I need to be
part of a storm
any storm
wanting it to happen
walking under it

But the cloud
full of dark promise
refuses to let go
like the teenaged girl
whose child's birth
is overdue

She plans to
give up her baby
in the tall evening grass
where the children
keep on looking
for their God

Afraid of Standing Still

Endangered by nothingness
We need to ascend —
In my balloon
I pass by a pedestal —
Under my hat
I discover a halo

Watch out for halos
In all this nothingness —
Buy a new hat
It will help you ascend —
Construct a pedestal
Hold the balloon

She waves the balloon
Blowing the halo
Right off the pedestal
Leaving me nothingness
Slowly ascending
Topped by a hat

That silly hat
Like the balloon
Dreams of ascending
Pretends it's a halo —
Surrounded by nothingness
It lands on a pedestal

You on your pedestal
In a straw hat —
Catch up to nothingness
Locate a balloon
Encourage the halo
Watch it ascend

How stubbornly we ascend
Past marble pedestals
Unreal as a halo
Is to a hat —
Don't let the balloon
Intrude on nothingness

Nothingness keeps on ascending
A balloon falls off a pedestal
Hatlesss I look for a halo

EVE

I was a made-to-order bride.
At first I didn't know Eden was beautiful
having nothing to compare it to,
but we were never hungry or afraid.
The sky was blue like Adam's eyes.

Adam and I played hide and seek
with lions or crawled along
the forest floor with snakes,
their secrets hissing in our ears,
the one about the tree of knowledge.

Its fruit appealed to us
because it was forbidden,
but eating it left us dissatisfied.
We saw each other redefined
in the surface of a lake.

That day a door slammed
in the sky. The monkeys cried,
the trees were shivering. —
The storm rolled us downhill,
blew us across a desert.

Growing up without adults
in a historic spotlight
I never learned to be
obedient, to differentiate
between adventure and sin.

Why was God so angry?
Did he regret creating me
neither puppet nor sheep?
Did he assume a little knowledge
would harm his fragile world?

In Transit

They wait their turn
In the castle
Of the yet unborn
Sleepy and scared

In the castle
Hidden by leaves
Sleepy and scared
Children in a valley

Hidden by leaves
The train stops briefly
In the valley
Of the day before

The train stops briefly
The sunshine
Of the day before
No longer relevant

The sunshine
Like fleeing armies
No longer relevant
Windows of sleep

Like fleeing armies
Seasons flash by
Windows of sleep
Recurring images

Seasons flash by
Out of control
Recurring images
A wind undresses a tree

Out of control
The yet unborn
A wind undresses a tree
They wait their turn

THE DOOR

No room
for one
more
generation —
Guarding
the door
of over-
crowded
Heaven
the dead
no longer
feel secure

Rumors About Heaven

1
There are these rumors
about heaven. The rumbling
in the sky before a storm
is inmates playing war games
to keep from being bored.

Do we grow young again
after we die?

2
Sometimes I like being a soldier,
sometimes I'm afraid.
The enemies are catching up
like violent shadows.

We are the good guys,
do as we are told,
good guys stuck in a game.

3
Last night Danny held my hand.
"I'll stay with you," he said
"so you won't get lost."

But earlier that day
a toy gun aimed at me
and he, beguiling
in a policeman's hat

"Aren't you a cop?" I said.
"No, I'm the bad guy now
and you are dead."

FAIRY TALE UPDATE

The Birthday Book

This storm won't go away
shares a room with a man
on the other side of the hill

The man can't hear
The storm outshouts the street

Climbing and sliding down
the man watches a cloud
in the shape of a goat

The storm watches the man
loading a gun

He still plays with his toys
A drawer opens years ago
New snow obscures his name

in the birthday book
the February page —

A Paved Forest

When Hansel and Gretel
set out to pick berries
in a paved forest
they lost their way
among the neon lights —
Back home their stepmother

had taken off her kerchief
releasing frustrated desires
she flew away —
The witch's candy house
waited where it always was
at the end of the prayer

Sometimes the pavement
turned into mirrors
inhabited by bells
Sometimes the captured children
saw their own shadows
looking for someone else

Sometimes they were allowed
to eat the candy
laced with crack
in the shape of hearts —
but eating never
left them satisfied

One day a weed grew
through a crack
in the witch's pavement —
That day the witch
crashed her erratic broom
over Arabia

To accommodate
an army of
transparent deer
and homeless stars
the weed became a tree
the tree turned into forests —

Hansel and Gretel
followed the smell of berries
on their way home.

Mary's House

for Mary Ferrari

I keep thinking
about Mary's house
ruled by the spirit
of freed green Africa.
Carefully painted
country style foreign
everything in it
has been transformed.

Don't let the makeup artist
repress your ego.
Don't cut your face
out of the photo.
Don't change places
with the imprisoned hero
before you know
how it ends

In a mansion
or a threatened garden
a confrontation
with an evil gang?
During this drought
it is important
to buy more shutters
and paint them green.

Dry Spell

A blue jay has hidden the key
that unlocks the sky

Flowers are wilted yet hopeful
The wind surrounding them
can't manage —

Weathermen prefer the sun
dole out the heat
bemoan a nonexistent storm

not the frustration of
locked clouds
the need for tears —

I'm thinking of someone
encased in my locket
unable to move

Behind a window of eyes
in black and white
he holds his breath

Ice Trees

It storms all night.
Among delicate ice trees,
each branch enclosed by mirrors,
the groom trying to reach the bride —

The bride's mother consults
two books of etiquette.
Gowns and napkins must be blue or white.
No drinks are served to thaw the guests.
Two upset grandmothers wear the same dress.

More clouds arrive.
Then all stand still for the photographer,
the ice-imprisoned trees,
the nervous bride
straining to please her mother.

White makes the bride look sad.
The groom likes the blue wind. —
When will the melting start?
What will fall and who will walk away?

Cradle Song

A light falls from the sky
and turns into a fish.
A golden fin of the fish
is the face of the moon.
A baby falls into a field

of words. First lesson,
how to fall. Follow a squirrel
towards a canopy of clouds —
The child lets go.
The squirrel falls asleep.

Fall into line.
Don't fall behind.
Take off your fairytale uniform.
No sense to fall in battle
unless you believe in a cause.

Don't fall for the wrong guy,
the one with nightfall eyes.
Avoid the falling waves,
hair falling like
confusing music.

There are no locks.
Fall flowers come and go.
A waterfall inspires them.
A light falls from the sky
and turns into a fish.

Threatened By Toys

At first I screened them,
let them in slowly,
but when they multiplied
they conquered every corner
of my mind.

The new police car
is too loud, too big.
A whole fleet of cars
lines up against me.
The sirens flash.

A too sophisticated doll
refuses to be held.
Three naked babies
piled up on one another
cry for their juice.

I'm wearing handcuffs
in my living room.
(The jail extends
across the street.)
When I try to escape
a vulture flies from the wall
and bites my leg.

I close a book.
Its stories follow me.
"Hey, don't ignore us.
Respect our rights."

More cars arrive.
(One driver is
a puppet without eyes.)
They speed into the woodwork.

The puppets wear the faces
of my enemies.
The rescue truck won't
rescue me. No room
to hide — I grow
smaller and smaller.

Constant Danger

1
In an unfurnished dollhouse
the newly arrived family
has no place to sleep.
They keep sliding off the roof
in constant danger
of being stepped upon
or led astray.

2
I worry too much about the people
I love. When they're out of reach
I imagine their balancing act
along the edge of the world.
Later they yell at me
and I feel reassured
for one more day.

3
When I sit up the small
boy says, "She is not dead"
and keeps on shooting.
In the background Tosca's lover
after his mock execution
is covered with real blood
can't walk away.

Catherine's Forest

Remembering Catherine Murray

As if this threatening forest
Were her jail
All pleasant pastel images
Dissolve and fail

She must lie still
And can't communicate
Leaves and sparrows have escaped
The tree trunks wait

Drugged worms are fastened
To a maple tree
A cloud is wheeled
Across the sky

She thinks of flight
All winter long
Strange women turn her over
Dark gods play with her tongue

Tower Door

1
Today consists of exits
and entrances.

Are these flesh-colored pants
or the old woman's legs?

She's gone inside.
We'll never know.

A stairway leads into
the tower of a hollow tree

then back into reality.
She follows the path

to where the play
did not take place.

2
The lions on location
or the woods surrounding them —

Which comes first?
You enter a plane

and exit in heaven.
You play a part

turn back into yourself
and take a bow.

3
The old woman
lives in the turret

of a linden tree
with phantom owls

behind green doors.
Having taken all her

vitamins she speeds by
on a motorcycle.

This time she wears a helmet
and suede boots.

Inside the hollow tower
a door slams shut.

A light goes on —

The Window Washer

Windows are barriers
between what's real
and what seems real

a cat through glass
a window washer
afraid of heights

Suspended on
the twenty-second floor
he tries to climb back in

The indoor cat looks out
A sudden hurricane
opens an eye

The ghosts of our bad deeds
look for an opening
Avoid them if you can

A Private Plane

Tonight I am vulnerable
as if I were sitting
in a private plane
piloted by an enemy.

He gives me a polluted smile.
The wind blows wilting
landmarks into my lap,
and the moon escapes.

Tonight I am expendable
on the way to a distant city
where someone tosses out a necklace
not made of gold.

The necklace once belonged to me.
I thought the one I gave it to
had liked it, thought I would
find traces of our journey.

Winter Interval

We travel so fast the moon is left
behind. The stars turn into lighted
windows, each with a story of its own.
Violetta, Tosca, the man next door.
The dying people sing.

A farmer reveals plans
for his fifteen future children.
Debbie's past and present boyfriends
ski side by side till there is no
more room in the family photo.

The wind keeps talking to the horses,
a breathlessness across the ice,
an unsteady half-smile.
Two by two my favorite people
wave to me on their way up.

Scenes from a Wedding

1
An uninhabited old mansion
overlooks the ocean. In two months
they will live there for three days.

A wedding elsewhere might
be more predictable,
but it's too late. The couple is
intrigued by ghosts.

Endless corridors, porcelain tubs,
gently peeling pastel walls,
a faded lawn in need of flowers.

Once there, they will detain the hours,
swing music converting halls.
Ancestral spirits, rudely awakened
will chant orders to caterers.

But food won't seem important when
bride and groom, a rabbi and a moon —
Is that Venus windsurfing?

2
The moment of arrival
its many windows lit.
Wildflowers everywhere
from forests, dawns
and endless halls
of a past century
are caught up in the dancing.
Rays of the setting sun
walk down the aisle
afraid of missing something
the wind so loud
the bride and groom
a brother and a poodle
all creatures of the earth
jump up into the arms
of a new symphony.

3
The lawn   the love   the haunted
mansion, the flowers in a row
all lean in one direction,
fly backwards through the sky.

As time goes on
the bedroom of the mind
becomes more sparsely furnished,
incomplete scattered images,
an eye without a face,
a fox above a house
listening, a dried bouquet.

It seems a guardian angel
withdrew after the wedding
causing guests to quarrel
on the way home. —
For a moment we were perfect,

each petal of each flower,
each nuance of the wind.
Even the shadows danced.

Witches Passing By

This forest has
an air of expectation,
left-over forest dwellers
covered with dew.

Their stories
just beyond the clearing,
almost accessible
the spell of pines.

The trees keep running
past the train.
They wave their arms
to ward off foul events.

Each time a storm
uproots a fir
a fairytale member
escapes. Which path

leads to the nightmare?
He hides under the table
of the rain.
Will he meet a moose?

Will he pass by
the love story of owls?
Will he catch a glimpse
of the restricted sun?

SELECTED POEMS

From RAPUNZEL (1971)

FRANCES

More than the lack of them it is
her inability to hold on
to things, her own stories
even; the family is always
breaking them. That day
the cat ate rat poison
and her sister burned the hair
off the doll. Then Frances wore
her cousin's glasses all weekend.

The Woods

Nothing is ordinary any more,
not the goose at my feet
that I close my eyes to,
not the candy wrapper flying away
with leaves. How can my appetite
be garden and gold?
They're aiming flashlights at us
from the woods.
Your face is like a weather map,
but even as I notice
and sitting next to you
I am too busy with required things.

The Tower

I brought you water in jail;
but water was not
enough.

Unable to cheer you up
or let you out
I locked myself in
being you.

Then you were glad that you had
other friends.

Rapunzel

At first you barely smiled,
then when I said good-bye
you said "hello
how have you been"
remembering
in the wrong act.
How much do you remember?
Does the tower have windows?
Are you obeying orders?
What do you see?
How dim you are, how rigid.

As Well As Nights

No stars tonight. Three street lamps
shine at regular intervals
too far apart for their circles
of light to touch.

Rapunzel   Rapunzel
Relinquish your tower.
The woods are paved,
The witch's spells are dated
And there are stars in you
As well as nights.

The Weekend

The rented bicycles gleamed across the bridge.
Lil led the way with her sailor Jim
and that medical student, handsome, rich
but dull, I think, I can't recall his name.
She'd dug him up for me before she knew
that I'd asked Tony. "Is it really true?"
his doctors teased. "Then you will have to bring
him home by stretcher." But it was he
      who carried me
almost, when I was out of breath uphill
and the others already out of sight.
"Come on!" he called and pushed my bike until
darkness seemed new again. I wondered why.
"Which of the lights is ours for the night?"
Jim fixed the flashlight to inquire by
when Lil's maps failed, and Tony read aloud.

Return by boat. On deck Lil cornered me.
"Having fun? But next time don't bring Tony.
He looks a mess and he is such a jerk."
Then later between sunset and New York
I went in search of what I thought I'd
missed among the others. Back from the pier
my bicycling improved. "How well I ride!"
to Tony who looked pale
and sank into the subway out of sight.
I realized then that he was rather nice.
What was left of us dressed for the night
to dine and dance at the Enchanted Nile.
My legs ached awfully. Lil said "please try."
With stilted conversation though in style
we tried to finish what had passed us by.

From
ONE-ARMED FLYER (1976)

December Street Scene

Along the littered street newly planted trees
(the last batch died)
and undernourished German shepherd strays
some sentimental
                music from a record store
                                    drifts to
        the butcher's door
where two pigs with their stomachs slit
are hanging upside down

dark Christmas angels

near the subway stop
that old man feeds

a frankfurter
to a stray dog.

Unlikely Marriage

In the dusty dollhouse
John Ashbery and Emily Dickinson
man and wife
have been asleep for years
with their six children
(one is lost)
that won't grow up
assorted dogs and cats
a wooden mouse and artificial flowers

In their colonial bed
turned to each other
they look uncomfortable.
Picasso prints are pasted on the walls

(The real John Ashbery
with a moustache
may not like
Dickinson's life style;
but here they are. They have no choice)

After an interlude
of climbing ladders and being hugged
they wait
he in a flannel suit
she with long hair
their arms outstretched

for the next generation.
A glass of plastic beer
on the red kitchen table
and manuscripts.

The Way You Are

I wanted to grow up the way you are
But now you're old. I'm leaving you behind
In a pink nursing home tied to a chair.

What's left of you can only shake and stare.
You bite the nurse and push away my hand.
I wanted to grow up the way you are.

I loved your gentleness and lack of fear
But what I loved I cannot find
In a pink nursing home tied to a chair.

Helpless I mourned your many deaths before
The final one. You used to understand
I wanted to grow up the way you are.

No one converses any more.
Each patient fights his private fiend
In a pink nursing home tied to a chair.

The silence in this day-room is bizarre.
You are alone, abandoned at the end
In a pink nursing home tied to a chair.
I wanted to grow up the way you are.

LULLABY

for my mother

Sun patterns on the wall.
The cat relaxes
in the fruit bowl.
   When I was small
you took me skiing every year
remember?
in love with speed
and reckless
younger than my father
who watched us from a deck chair
in the sun
and has not aged since then.
   You have.
When you are dead
I'll have you back again
the way you were.

From
JOURNEYS AROUND
ONE POINT (1980)

Young Girl Sleeping Late

And still she sleeps
near windows where the sun —
it's five p.m. —
on his way out
glows hauntingly

Pillow with stripe of sun
light ivory.
She wears a woolen hat
all day in bed
to flatten her hair

From a space
behind the painted lashes
exotic night
plans penetrate this sleep,
and the sun
above the dark-edged quilt
wears himself out.

Sailboat

1
It's the light that turns
us around
blue in the mirrored room.
Some people close their eyes.

some people arm in arm
in boats
forgetful of a future
— *haven't seen you   how come?*

Small plastic sailboats take the longest
		journeys —
blue flowers on the shore —
When Andrew sinks them they
arise again.

2
Why am I always writing about sailboats?
was in one only once
invited by my cousin and his girl
out of a sense of obligation.

Uneasy   bored
I listened to their private overtures
in the sailboat   in the wind
I was in love
and he was at the beach.

Those days I felt invulnerable
once swam way out —
Carried sideways by the current
I reached another section of the shore,
had to walk back for miles.

The teacher got hysterical
at our beach.
Big boys who'd never noticed me
became aware.

Arriving unobserved I joined the crowd —
lifeboats rowed out
to the horizon — looking for me.
I said, *What are we doing?*

★ ★ ★ ★ ★ ★

6
One by one windows light up —
the nightsky an untouched blue —
three streetlamps point the way
to what we may become.

I grew up with the painting
of a sailboat on the wall
surreal in a lake of dots,
grew to love it, gave it away
to a girl and boy who never look

This painting
under a special light
the boat seems to be gliding
back and forth.

I call a clerk
to ask about my mother —
our paper ships turned over
we used to cross the river
barefoot from rock to rock —
her mind went first.

One day
a wind just right
the boat will sail again,
the girl and boy will redirect their eyes.

7
Some nights a brightness that is not
the moon
the whiteness of a sailor ghost
(we travel in our sleep)
bleaches the horizon

But from a distance
when we're awake
the people who adjust the sheets
who scrub the deck
look at the sky
in many languages
are never visible

only slow moving sails
like prehistoric birds

From
THE CROSSING (1984)

Pack of Dogs

dark dogs, one has
a broken chain around
his neck and a sore paw.
smaller than the
others, he lags behind

it happened weeks ago:
phantoms breaking away
from a May night.
they follow one another
aimlessly
down the street
as if together
they're no longer lost
among the blossoms of
this sudden heat

men are sent out
to hunt for them
trust no one — run —
they hide   we hide
a jungle of neat houses —
run away

Imagined Rain

Always it was the distant cloud
with its elusive lies
that signaled   *come*
the lights in foreign towers
in the dark teacher's eyes.

The one who wanted to sit next
to me was never as appealing
as those in other boats
or those who swam away
into another story.

I used to say *why didn't you* —
you used to say *I'm here*.
Now you reside on the top floor
not listening (I shout and shout)
or with your back to me
in your pajamas
as if you hadn't died.

Colonial Doll House

1
Carried through real wind
and up the stairs to be assembled
before the story
can begin.

2
Jessica liked the doll house
better before she owned it.

3
Endlessly we fasten shingles.

4
"Why are you always thinking
of my house?" she says

5
Tom Bodenhauser has moved in. Outside
it rains but nothing penetrates.

6
Eliza, his new wife from Germany
is placed into his bed
without a wedding.

7
His other wife has been beheaded.

8
He teaches history.

Doll Houses

1
In doll houses at night
children don't mature
each moment lasts
until a hand lifts them up —
the hand wears silver rings

2
All year
their clocks stand still

the mother sleeps
the baby doesn't drink

men with moustaches
from another time

who never argue
never age

but when the house
is turned around

under their paintings
of themselves

their shadows grow —

* * * * *

7
When everyone moves away
she buys a set of dishes
intensely blue
like rural mountain lakes

all sorts of other objects
assert themselves
the profile
winks at her, a lamp
is growing roots —

birds have captured the window.
above her head a row of tired dancers.
hear the slow exit
of the snow —

From
CALENDAR HOUSE (1990)

Painted Windows

Artists are hired
to paint the windows
of abandoned buildings
in the South Bronx.
Storm clouds keep filing

past armed guards
and pastel images —
Once I liked the witch's house
and Spanish houses
painted on the set
of Verdi's opera
— Rodrigo in his armor
Don Carlo in despair
The Grand Inquisitor intends
to burn them all —

Imagine owning nothing after the fire
while your apartment
the one you used to live in
shows neatly painted shutters
and simulated smiles.

All winter feelings flare
and cars pass by.
Like homeless people
old leaves fly up to haunt
their former trees.

Calendar House

1
The house in the painting
is too pretty,
broken shingles hidden by leaves.
The reds are too red
the yellows too yellow
trapped on the October page
of a calendar.

2
What if the colors fade
along the outskirts of the canvas —
What if a storm develops on
the upper right —
What if the seasons change
but not inside the garden
of this house —

3
The storm affects
the couple in the house.
It makes them wish and fear to be
a part of it.

4
The woman runs out of the house
towards the storm.
You see her back and one foot
lifted slightly.

5
The house is still unfurnished.
When uninvited relatives arrive
the door slams shut.

6
The unused upstairs waits
for a future, rose-painted
ceilings, a balcony —

From the basement
boxes of wooden eagles
and rusty knife blades call
Inherit me.

7
The house takes off.
It floats above
a war zone near a village —

The woman's frozen
in a running pose
a few feet from the house.

8
To give the house a new dimension
repaint it violet.
Release the running woman from the canvas.
Make them rake up their leaves.

The Semiconscious Bride

The earth is asleep —
On this dangerously cold December
don't go out
rock in your rocking chair
cover up with dreams

The homeless will be
rounded up and sung to
the strays will be adopted
the soldiers will not die

While the president's heart
goes out to them all
the rest of his body
resumes its hunting trip

In distant alley-windows
and hidden lakes
reflecting flags
someone is always
killing someone else

My TV program's
always interrupted
I get annoyed
not having tuned into reality —
yet the newscast won't go away

In the streets
of another country
where new troops keep arriving
every day
a disoriented former lover
rediscovers his voice

"Let fictional characters
take over the world

Repaint the electric chair
in pastel colors

Restore the rainforest
on your way to kissing
the semiconscious bride."

From
ENEMY ON THE WAY
TO SCHOOL (1994)

The Island

First formal dance in England:
We fell in love in quicksand.
Too young to take a stand
We smiled and closed our eyes.

Too young to take a stand
We saw sharks in disguise
And ships that tried to land.
We smiled and closed our eyes.

And ships that tried to land
Were taken by surprise.
Ghosts led us by the hand
Said, smile and close your eyes.

Ghosts led us by the hand
Grownups who once seemed wise.
Their murders were preplanned.
Just smile and close your eyes.

Their murders were preplanned.
Tucked in on an island
We grew up in quicksand
And smiled and closed our eyes.

HIGH HOLY DAY

On Yom Kippur I feel
left out.
People around me
are dressed up.
So are their children's dolls.
I light a candle, don't
fast, see Dallas.

The leaf I touch has not
yet turned. Will next year's
earth be safe?
All this is written down
and sealed today.

I'm thinking of the girl
in the photo
(the mother-in-law I never knew)
deported to a Polish ghetto.
Did she learn to pray
or die for a religion
she did not believe in?

No lake to throw my sins into
only stirred up circles
in the puddle
of pale leaves shining
like injured angels.

Where Dragons Sang

1
What I remember has
no beginning and no walls.
each fragment hangs like a cloud
without a sky. slowly
as I practice the
piano, a crystal chandelier
falls from the cloud
slowly it keeps on
falling like snow —

2
I can recall
a door that didn't open
a child I wouldn't
play with, the play I missed
not what I kept on seeing
through the window
(blue out of nowhere, suns
out of sequence) thinking
I'll always remember this

the door was on a mountain
the play about a virgin
who chopped off someone's head —
when the carriage overturned
the child I wouldn't play with
picked up my four dolls
from the grass spitefully
left me an evil image of myself.

3
Now I'm walking backwards on
this German avenue (I feel quite
safe) in boots under a narrow
moon, past the mysterious fire —
walking to where my mother
knew I loved her
to where the Stürmer printed
lies on giant columns on every
street — a Jew with crooked nose and
evil eyes. some boys
cornered me—
walking to where our dog hid from
the birthday party where dragons sang
and shadows carried guns
to where the *Nibelungen,*
the wronged dwarfs —
I stepped on the white berry
made a popping sound. the lady in the
moss house drifted down the river.
I held four dolls. Siegfried revived
his dragon. the streetsigns marched
saluted, turned around

Marianne

Years later I came across her
German letters, assertive, questioning
written in '37
after six months of strolling:
a Berlin schoolyard, arm in arm.

Striving for some storybook
perfection we sent our lives
from Italy to England and
back again. There was that singer,
unrequited love, "quite normal at
our age," she said

remembering how we had once waited
for hours in a hallway
across the street from Dr. Löwenthal,
the teacher we had a crush on
who never got away.

Politics were, like paintings
in our houses, important only when
one looked at them. We looked
at new lights on the edge of seas.
One day all those events
will step out of their frames.
Married one day we won't know
each other's names.

MEMORIAL TO THE MOON

Third Act

Secrets are brought to
the surface. The actors
are drowning in light.

When will the curtain close?
Help, I'm growing ugly.
Is God still directing?

Homesick for whispers and waves
imprisoned in act three
I forget my exit line.

In old movies it is clear
when a story winds down.
The moon moves closer

to the river,
the music grows louder,
large letters say, THE END.

Phyllis's Funeral

So many hiding places in a clock,
so many numbers, pauses, passageways.

To avoid the funeral I play hide
and seek in a meadow in Italy.
The moon wears a white coat and finds me.

I call a number. It still plays her voice.
The voice is homeless now yet reassuring.
"Leave a message. I'll get back to you."

Chemo Marathon

1
Good and bad knights battle in my veins.
A raccoon believes he owns the forest.
A tycoon has lost his hair.
On a disintegrating field
knights do each other in.

2
A cockroach frightens Mary Stuart
in the tower, shortly
before her execution.
It is futile to keep chasing
cockroaches or crowns.

3
Death and hope walk through the
forest, making bets. The tycoon
is never happy. The raccoon
still wears white socks. Together
they drift backwards to beginnings.

Prelude to a Beheading

In order to shut out the guillotine
I contemplate a festive crowd.
Children are led through falling snow
To learn about the fallen heads.

I contemplate a festive crowd,
Await my turn, pray to my God.
To learn about the fallen heads
Wild shadows overwhelm the sky.

I wait my turn, pray to my God.
Don't let it hurt too terribly.
Wild shadows overwhelm the sky.
An old man waves a flag and shouts.

Don't let it hurt too terribly.
It isn't my fault I was rich.
An old man waves a flag and shouts
"Death to all aristocrats!"

It isn't my fault I was rich
In a gold palace, young, in love.
"Death to all aristocrats!"
It has stopped snowing. No more clouds.

In a gold palace, young, in love
Children are led through falling snow.
It has stopped snowing. No more clouds
To shut out the guillotine.

Sonata

Unending music can be a rebuff.
He loved her too, but not enough.

When he took the plunge into unbeing
She found another way of seeing

The earth as a rehearsal space,
The moon with an artistic face.

ABSENCE 2

I dreamed you many times
after you died,
dreamed you impatient,
re-dreamed you kind,
re-lost you every dawn.

You challenge
the impossible, drive me
to music festivals
in cosmic caravans.

The endless, restless
music of your mind —
I fail you nightly
so I am left behind,
re-lost at dawn.

Assistant Gods

The world has grown
too complex for one God.
Among the words and winds,
the sins and seeds,
the birds and clouds
live the assistant gods.

Often unnoticed, the miracles
are countless and haphazard,
stars returned to the sky,
souls rescued from a jar.

Assistant gods rule in
confusion. Heroes turn
into villains on a whim.
The dead protect the living,
heal their dreams.

The world has grown
too complex for one God.
People praying come to see
that they are not alone.
A wing, a wind, a lantern
where an assistant god

saves lives, all but his own.
Wayward hymns confound
the sky. A star escapes
from a book to enter an eye.

The Album

Nobody bothered to
write down their names.

How well they ski, these two.
Are they in love? Is that
a pregnant wife, a jealous aunt?
How elegant their clothes,
how steep the snow!

A taxi driver drops me off
in the middle of that snow
held captive by one moment.
He has a terrifying face.
No landmarks look familiar.

Shortly before he died
I asked my father who they were,
the people in his photo album,
but he too had forgotten.

Memorial to the Moon

Ready or not, here it comes —

The moon goes underground.
Veiled flowers run and hide.
The stars wear masks.
The mountains are disguised.

A man becomes invisible
airborne yet vulnerable
(yellow face
of a small bird).

Candles flicker for miles
for all things I can't find —
Let's have a memorial service.

WATERCOLORS

Snow-covered mountains
and one small boat.
The mountains run away.
The boat stands still,
orange and unoccupied.

Mountains holding hands
reflected in a lake
from faint green spring
to deep green forest
to white eternity.

The lake is empty like
a mind with no memories.
They've sailed away.
Snow-covered mountains
and one small boat.

OUTLINES

Over there on the horizon
that may not be a brown bag
but a blond child. His birthday
is the day my husband died.
The brown bag is carried by
a father's shadow, or a wind
holds the hand of the child.

Family Tree

In some gardens time
lags behind. Ancestors
and future children
line up on the lawn.

Across the street
falling apart
under a flowering cloud
floats a small house.

Intense shadows ring
the bell. Ambitions
sway in the wind.
"What about us?"

Frail leaves have given up.
Flowing like bloodstreams
towards a heart
the branches write new poems.

Ceremonies in White

1
Whiter than wedding gowns,
brighter than street lamps
the moon rolls down
from the sky, sits on a curb
eating cheesecake —

a whole cake. He devours it
all at once without a fork
as if stolen or forbidden,
devours it like the old
consuming their last moments.

By the time the wedding cake
is served, the guests are full.
They risk a stomach ache
but can't resist. The bride,
too excited to eat

rises up into the sky
dressed as the moon.

2
Six bridesmaids wearing black.
One spring night dressed in snow.

The roses look unreal,
their opulent perfection
in the middle of a war.
Giddily we leap in circles,
plan to rebuild the cities
we destroy. All night
the bride can't stop smiling.
A flower girl won't stop dancing,
the other one asleep
on the outskirts of the band.

Cameras catch everyone,
wedding guests arriving,
soldiers recovering,
the couple lifted high,
so temporary, so promising —

Six bridesmaids wearing black.
One spring night dressed in snow.

To a Teenager

How much of you takes root
depends on what you wish

and where you look,
which petals will unfold,

turn a beguiling blue
while the sky in search

of an elusive star
is kneeling in the mud.

The landscape is fenced off.
Carefully crafted words

bounce off the fence unheard.
On one side an empty lot,

on the other, in a sea of green
the persuasive trees.

Drought

A sunbeam
pierces a butterfly
on its way to a wedding
in a wilted bouquet.

A mute violinist
sits in an orchestra,
raises his instrument,
but nothing happens.

The children walk along
streets of their music,
one drum and four guitars
without an audience.

They're wishing for
a rain adventure
inside a gloomy nightmare
far from school.

How cool and dark it is,
how reassuring.
The sky wakes up refreshed
from a long sleep.

Visit

A poem arrives at my window
stands on a ledge looking in.
A cat tries chasing it.

Magical and frail
the poem stands firm.
The cat goes crazy.

Time out. A moon surveys
the scene. The cat gets tired
of hitting the screen.

The sky looms upside down.
The day is turned around.
The spirits fly away —

Revolving Door

A house with a round door
is what I've always wanted,
the future, past and present
inside out. This morning

Mary Stuart was beheaded,
an astronaut entered the moon
and Anna brought the baby
to show and tell.

The actors have reinvented
the play, moved it
closer to Broadway.
Now the scenery takes over

and a real window opens
for the hero to escape.
It overlooks the past,
always someone else's past

turns out to be your own.
Spotlights clarify the
journey towards an ending
and the backstage God.

Inside-Out

In a dollhouse under
A painting of mountains
A woman is sleeping,
Her husband not nearby.
The shadow of a squirrel,
A dissolving dream
Begins to climb a tree.
Glimpses of many heavens,
The mountain in the painting,
The painting in the dollhouse,
The husband on his way.

Notes on Growing Up

1
I am special, can do no wrong.
But sometimes parents go away
and it gets dark.

2
Every night I reinvent God
out of cloud formations and my
own needs. Sometimes I pray.

3
I'm obsessed with heroes,
afraid of fortune tellers.
They predict a long life.
How disappointing. I'll be
too old to die young.

4
The moment of the garden party
on the first day of school
I find out that I'm Jewish
and not well liked.

5
I move into the dollhouse.
A Victorian family waits for me there.
We lead a full, imaginary life.

6
I am Joan of Arc.
Circumstances and perception
have created me. Villains in
one country are heroes in another.

7
I give up on heroism,
decide to settle for the ordinary.
Instead of reaching thousands
I concentrate on three.

8
In my spare time I collect
moments, put them in a box,

the moment of the missing cat
climbing out of a flower bed,
the moment of a concert in a meadow,
the moment of the promise I can't keep.

9
Every day I feel lucky and sad.
Blue river flowers in the path
of Hitler on the way to now.

Tree Shadows

Thunder and midnight rain.
"Hey kid, go home"
to a book in a room, a crow's
nest, a recurring voice.

A young man slinks along
edges of flower beds
towards the linden tree,
stays there for hours.

He lights a cigarette.
From side to side his arms
and branches sway. It storms
relentlessly. Only
the tree-trunk stays calm.

I get ready for bed.
The boy's still there.
Does he contemplate
suicide, robbery or
the rain? From time to time
he and the sky light up.

Lightning intensifies
the anger of the sky.
Bursts of smoke from an
invisible mouth.

"Hey kid, run away.
There's danger under
the linden tree. Go home!"

Basement Mirror

Down narrow stairs
that shift and turn
the frail couple
in each other's eyes
see what they wish to see
(silver napkin rings
intriguing teas)
he behind dark glasses
she among eternal iris

The Lamp Breaks

The lamp breaks easily
wears out from too much use.
When it is lit the words smile
on the page. Everything's clear
under my lamp, the one with the golden
lines.

When the lamp breaks, the eyes forget.
Stories retreat beneath the bed.
Over the phone at 4 A.M.
a stranger whispers, *It is time* —
and in the lampless room nobody smiles.

When you leave, turn off the light.
The lamp breaks easily.
The wires fray, bulbs burn out
till no one finds his way except the cat
looking for fireflies and giddy stars.

A Shelter Story

He has a key to nowhere.
Ideas jump up, fall over.
His shadow can't keep up.

It has to do with challenges
and getting bored. It has to do
with not finding a way.

Disappointed mentors
and elusive flowers
collide in a tug of war.

He knows he's brilliant,
likes the sound of his disease,
makes up a song about it.

Reclassified

When wildflowers were
Reclassified
Some men sprayed pesticide
And called them weeds.

Reclassified
The earth went into shock.
Deprived of weeds
It slept a hundred years.

The earth went into shock
In a dismantled garden.
It slept a hundred years
Dreaming of dandelions.

In a dismantled garden
Used by ambitious orphans
Dreaming of dandelions
Transformed into gold crowns.

The ambitious orphans
Grew up to be bad poets,
Traded gold crowns
For moments without images.

Grew up to be bad poets
Spraying pesticide
On moments without images
Of wildflowers.

INTERLUDE

A soon-to-depart
and a recently-arrived
play together
in a living room.

The recently-arrived
still wears diapers
but can write her name.

The soon-to-depart
babysits for a bear,
an easy job she likes.

A double door.
The recently-arrived
in a straw hat
keeps walking in and out.

"Goodbye," she says.
"I have to go to work."

Casey the poodle
plays a minor part.
Tomorrow Erik will be
leaving for Australia.

The doors open and close.

Indoor Duet

(for Zoe)

Will she hunt in woods that I imagine?
Does my shadow enter her dreams?

We stare at each other, the cat and I,
communicate without revealing secrets.

In the street the snow is overflowing.
Everything's near, yet out of reach.

With her in my lap I can't read a book.
She can't catch the sparrow behind glass.

From separate spheres we take turns ignoring
each other until our moods converge.

Unblinking eyes the color of the Nile,
an unsolved sky, new footprints in the snow.

We watch each other asleep —

The Curtain

Worshiper, what do you worship?
The answer dwells behind the
curtain of the sky.

Worshiper, you are too busy
breathing and swallowing
to notice moongods among leaves.

Worshiper, you think you'll
enter heaven, not knowing heaven
is where you've been.

Call Waiting

Wilting forget-me-nots along
the shore. The boat is stuck,
the mood is blue, the moon
withdrawn from the river.

As soon as you hold
the blue flower the phone stops
ringing and someone places
cowbells in your ears.

A blue jay's banished from the sky.
It's not the cell phone
in the tower but the
conniving nun who put it there.

Is there something left to say,
someone to say it to?
Don't go into the wilderness
without your earrings.

The New Millennium

I don't want to go there —

I want to go backwards
into the forest
where the endangered hide

or to an unexplored moon
in an adventure story
from another time.

At the entrance hall
of the century
account numbers
illuminate the view,

an avalanche of people
wired together.
When I press a button
they dance in the street.

Fall 2001

Secretive storm clouds
terrorize the sky.

Indoctrinated men in caves
inhabit our minds.

Among leaves at a cemetery
obsolete rituals hide.

Diseases arrive in envelopes.
Poisonous flowers run wild.

The baby wears an American flag
and the cat on the sofa smiles.

STORYTELLER

A woman rushes by, hopeful, barefoot
and out of breath. This is the story-
teller. Her smile is on the screen.

A woman wades across the river.
The stones she steps on
to keep her balance
are variations of the truth.

Remembered forget-me-nots screen
a woman from the forest footnote,
altering the landscape's story.

A woman lies unconscious in her story.
I see a wounded skyline on a screen,
see myself, the way I drag my feet.

Blurred Flowers

A bridal couple from
another time
poses behind glass.
New buds have just begun.

Child suicide bombers —
A spring of few choices —
Only the flowers are real.

Carried to her house
still wrapped in mystery
she remembers nothing.
Her name is Emily

under the sky's
precarious first smile.

The bride has a leaf
on her forehead
and one open eye.
The other eye turns inward.

The groom looks bewildered
yet determined, like
soldiers killed in Iraq,
not quite grown up.

For Kathie

Some old people seek the sun
as if it won't recur,
not in their lifetime,
but I stay home
and rediscover Kathie.

The way her voice,
the way the spring
from distant spheres
repeats itself,
but never quite the same.

Open the door, and there
she is, carrying bags
of groceries for me.

Her words dispel evil spirits.
Her entrances marks the end
of local clouds.

Usually she's in a hurry.
The minutes run away
and I chase after them.
Let me keep this one
just a little longer.

WILDERNESS

All morning on a Utah mountain
an overcast sky holds back
the rain like ambushed tears.

In this wilderness
they force-feed values,
other people's values
when Dan would rather hang out
in the street equipped with money,
other people's money.

The storm breaks loose,
arrives full force. Surrounded
by deceptive mirrors Dan stands
on the edge of a steep cloud.

Will new voices get through?
Will his anger yield to
the mountains? Will he be
frightened? Will he hold on?
Will the sky clear?

PASSWORD

Panicky voices run back
and forth in time,

rock stars outsung
by prehistoric birds,
the voice of a forgotten king
trapped in a zoo

and now and then
a beleaguered lion roaring
lullabies to future cubs.

At one time there were
intervals of silence.

People managed to listen
to the sea, the wind,
the voice of God

telling Joan to lead an army,
Noah to build an ark
and Moses to leave Egypt
in a hurry.

I throw away the ailing
answering machine,
receive a secret password,

and a new moon
will tell me what to do

Heaven

I'm sitting in the lap
of my old age.
I do not like this part.
The casting is all wrong.
I try to run away but have no shoes.

Grandchildren on my dresser
grow and smile.
My mother in a silver frame
shadowy in black and white
looks after me, keeps me a child.

Mostly I pretend and sleep.
A wooden moose in moonlight
comes alive. Stories arrive,
and are carried off by a blue wind.
If heaven does exist I'll be surprised.

Gabriela

(for Andrew)

Perhaps eternity is not
endurance but recurrences,
leaves coming back in other
versions of themselves.

Perhaps God has more than one son,
all of them crucified,
all of them holy.

He also has a daughter
named Gabriela
at an orphanage in Peru.
She keeps searching for a family

the way new words
are searching for a story.
But it's too late.

A border has been crossed.
False drumbeats have led her away.

Rendezvous

Germans and desire merge
in this runaway dream.

Will it always be like this?
An oasis, an angelic sleep
eternally damned?

Her profession is on hold.
He's awaiting transportation
to an island colony.

At a hospital
a prostitute with syphilis
enters the room of a leper.

Gerry Waiting

He has been waiting for me
a long time, waiting underground.
He does not like it there.

Will he lead me to
the realm of non-existence
on a cloud that can't be
anchored or confirmed?
Will he show me around?

Or shall we be ashes together
landing on a flower?

The flower, one of many,
grows in a forest
on the edge of a river.
Small and intensely blue
it's called forget-me-not.

Being already forgotten
we won't understand that name.

ABOUT THE AUTHOR

Annette Hayn grew up in Germany during the early stages of the Nazi regime. In 1937 she was sent to a boarding school in Brighton, England, and in 1940 she and her parents emigrated to the United States.

She graduated from Columbia University and received the Bernice Kavinoky Isaacson award for poetry at The New School for Social Research.

She lived for many years in Queens Village, New York, where she was active in community theater and was affiliated with New York State Poets in the Schools. She had three children, and dedicated this final collection to her grand-daughter Anna.

About This Book

The type used in this book is Aldine, based on early typefaces created by Venetian printer Aldus Manutius, one of the great pioneering humanist printers and publishers. The headlines are set in Charlemagne and Calligraphic, two faces inspired by hand-lettering.

The book design is by Brett Rutherford, using digital photographs combined with other images of violins and classic doll houses.

The type has been reset for this second edition, and the section, *Memorial to the Moon,* is new to this edition. These are Annette Hayn's final poems.

www.ingramcontent.com/pod-product-compliance
Lightning Source LLC
Chambersburg PA
CBHW051652040426
42446CB00009B/1095